Notebook for Anna Magdalena Bach and Baritone Ukulele

Ondřej Šárek

Contents

Introductions 3
How to read tablature....................... 3
Menuet BWV Anh. 114. 4
Menuet BWV Anh. 115. 5
Menuet BWV Anh. 116. 8
Menuet BWV Anh. 118. 10
Polonaise BWV Anh. 119. 12
Menuet BWV Anh. 121. 13
Menuet BWV Anh. 120. 14
Aria BWV Anh. 515. 16
Musette BWV Anh. 118. 17
Menuet(not BWV) 18
Polonaise BWV Anh. 128. 20
Untitled Piece BWV Anh. 131. 21
Menuet BWV Anh. 132. 22

Copyright © 2012 Ondřej Šárek
All rights reserved.
ISBN-13: 978-1481077828
ISBN-10: 1481077821

Notebook for Anna Magdalena Bach and Baritone Ukulele 2

Introductions

Notebook for Anna Magdalena Bach belongs among most known didactic pieces for key instruments. There are famous compositions that where played on almost all instruments. You will find on internet even versions for ukulele. But in what is the difference within this collection and previous arrangements? This collection keeps original notation and furthermore the melody and the bass accompaniment (thus polyphony) is re-arranged for ukulele. Therefore, when you learn more difficult arrangement, you will be able to admire beauty of baroque polyphony.

Historical excursion:
Notebook for Anna Magdalena Bach exists in two versions. The first one comes from 1722 and the second one (with more compositions) is from 1725. All pieces in the version from 1722 were composed by Johann Sebastian Bach. For the second version is the compilation of works from several composers. It is such an example what Bach family could enjoy. Not always, it was possible to determine exactly, who composed what song. Therefore, the question mark can be found after the name. But somewhere it did. For the reason, do not be surprised when you will read that the most famous Minuet (BWV Anh.114) was not composed by Johann Sebastian Bach but by Christian Petzold.

How to read tablature

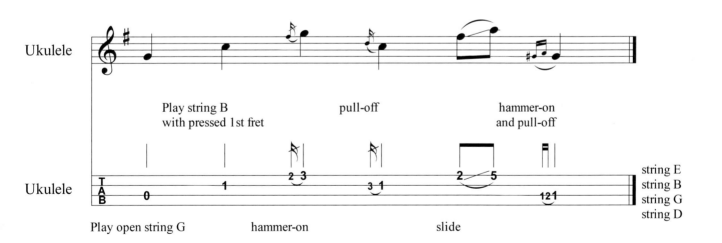

Menuet
BWV Anh. 114.

Christian Petzold
arr: Ondřej Šárek

Notebook for Anna Magdalena Bach and Baritone Ukulele 4

Menuet

Menuet

BWV Anh. 115.

Score

Christian Petzold
arr: Ondřej Šárek

Notebook for Anna Magdalena Bach and Baritone Ukulele 6

Menuet

Notebook for Anna Magdalena Bach and Baritone Ukulele 7

Menuet

BWV Anh. 116.

Score

unknown composer
arr: Ondřej Šárek

Notebook for Anna Magdalena Bach and Baritone Ukulele 8

Menuet

Notebook for Anna Magdalena Bach and Baritone Ukulele 9

Menuet
BWV Anh. 118.

Score

unknown composer
arr: Ondřej Šárek

Notebook for Anna Magdalena Bach and Baritone Ukulele

Menuet

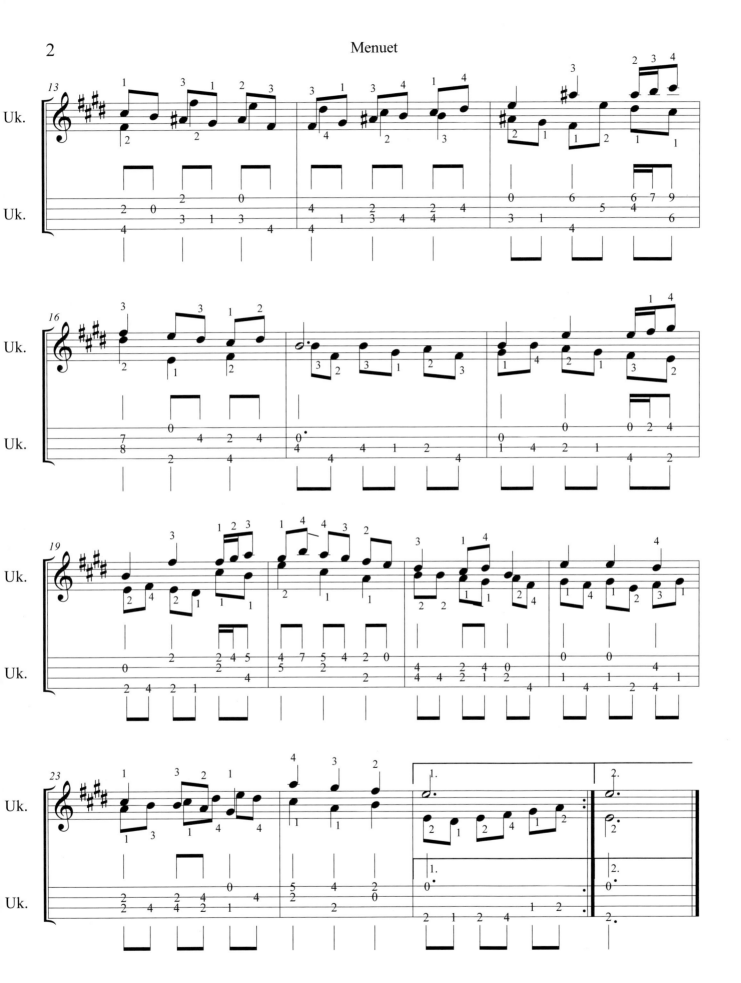

Notebook for Anna Magdalena Bach and Baritone Ukulele 11

Polonaise
BWV Anh. 119.

Score

unknown composer
arr: Ondřej Šárek

Notebook for Anna Magdalena Bach and Baritone Ukulele 12

Menuet
BWV Anh. 121.

unknown composer
arr: Ondřej Šárek

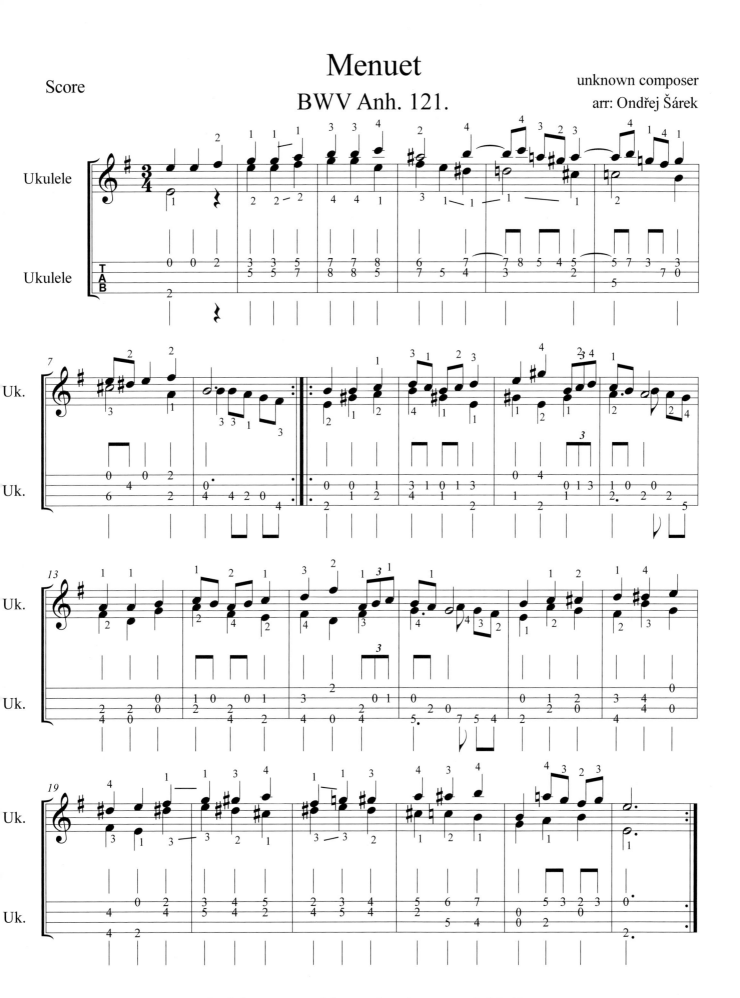

Notebook for Anna Magdalena Bach and Baritone Ukulele 13

Menuet
BWV Anh. 120.

unknown composer
arr: Ondřej Šárek

Notebook for Anna Magdalena Bach and Baritone Ukulele 14

Menuet

Musette
BWV Anh. 126.

unknown composer
arr: Ondřej Šárek

Score

Notebook for Anna Magdalena Bach and Baritone Ukulele 17

Menuet

Not included in the BWV catalogue.

Score

Georg Böhm
arr: Ondřej Šárek

Notebook for Anna Magdalena Bach and Baritone Ukulele

Menuet

Polonaise
BWV Anh. 128.

Score

unknown composer
arr: Ondřej Šárek

Notebook for Anna Magdalena Bach and Baritone Ukulele

Untitled Piece
BWV Anh. 131.

Gottfied Heinrich Bach ?
arr: Ondřej Šárek

Notebook for Anna Magdalena Bach and Baritone Ukulele 21

New ukulele books

For C tuning ukulele
Classics for Ukulele (Mel Bay Publications)
Ukulele Bluegrass Solos (Mel Bay Publications)
Antonin Dvorak: Biblical Songs (CreateSpace Independent Publishing Platform)
Irish tunes for all ukulele (CreateSpace Independent Publishing Platform)
Gospel Ukulele Solos (CreateSpace Independent Publishing Platform)
Gregorian chant for Ukulele (CreateSpace Independent Publishing Platform)
The Czech Lute for Ukulele (CreateSpace Independent Publishing Platform)
Romantic Pieces by Frantisek Max Knize for Ukulele (CreateSpace Independent Publishing Platform)
Notebook for Anna Magdalena Bach and Ukulele (CreateSpace Independent Publishing Platform)

For C tuning with low G
Irish tunes for all ukulele (CreateSpace Independent Publishing Platform)
Gospel Ukulele low G Solos (CreateSpace Independent Publishing Platform)
Antonin Dvorak: Biblical Songs: for Ukulele with low G (CreateSpace Independent Publishing Platform)
Gregorian chant for Ukulele with low G (CreateSpace Independent Publishing Platform)
The Czech Lute for Ukulele with low G (CreateSpace Independent Publishing Platform)
Romantic Pieces by Frantisek Max Knize for Ukulele with low G (CreateSpace Independent Publishing Platform)
Notebook for Anna Magdalena Bach and Ukulele with low G (CreateSpace Independent Publishing Platform)

For Baritone ukulele
Irish tunes for all ukulele (CreateSpace Independent Publishing Platform)
Gospel Baritone Ukulele Solos (CreateSpace Independent Publishing Platform)
Antonin Dvorak: Biblical Songs: for Baritone Ukulele (CreateSpace Independent Publishing Platform)
Gregorian chant for Baritone Ukulele (CreateSpace Independent Publishing Platform)
The Czech Lute for Baritone Ukulele (CreateSpace Independent Publishing Platform)
Romantic Pieces by Frantisek Max Knize for Baritone Ukulele (CreateSpace Independent Publishing Platform)
Notebook for Anna Magdalena Bach and Baritone Ukulele (CreateSpace Independent Publishing Platform)

For 6 sting ukulele (Lili'u ukulele)
Gospel 6 string Ukulele Solos (CreateSpace Independent Publishing Platform)
Gregorian chant for 6 string Ukulele (CreateSpace Independent Publishing Platform)
Notebook for Anna Magdalena Bach and 6 string Ukulele (CreateSpace Independent Publishing Platform)

For Slide ukulele (lap steel ukulele)
Comprehensive Slide Ukulele: Guidance for Slide Ukulele Playing (CreateSpace Independent Publishing Platform)
Gospel Slide Ukulele Solos (CreateSpace Independent Publishing Platform)
Irish tunes for slide ukulele (CreateSpace Independent Publishing Platform)

For D tuning ukulele
Skola hry na ukulele (G+W s.r.o.)
Irish tunes for all ukulele (CreateSpace Independent Publishing Platform)

Coming soon!

Jewish songs for ukulele (CreateSpace Independent Publishing Platform)
Notebook for Anna Magdalena Bach: Duet (CreateSpace Independent Publishing Platform)
Open Tunings for Ukulel (Mel Bay Publications)

Notebook for Anna Magdalena Bach and Baritone Ukulele 24

Made in United States
North Haven, CT
24 February 2022